WHAT NOT TO SAY AT A FUNERAL

An Unexpectedly Humorous Guide To Showing Up When It Matters Most

by

Amy Havis

EXPLORING UNCHARTED CREATIVITY
LEFT FIELD PUBLISHING
EST 2024
LITTLETON · COLORADO

COPYRIGHT

First published in the United States of America, October 2026
by Left Field Publishing.

ISBN: 9781966883128

This book reflects the author's personal experiences and perspectives. Names and identifying details of individuals have been changed in some cases to protect privacy. Any resemblance to actual persons or events beyond those explicitly identified is coincidental.

This book is intended for informational and reflective purposes only. It is not a substitute for professional medical, psychological, legal, or other expert advice. Readers are encouraged to seek appropriate professional guidance for their individual circumstances.

Library of Congress Control Number: 2026903921

Book Cover by Kristen Gilligan

DEDICATION

To Hope:

I miss you every day. I can't wait to see you again, when all things are made new.

To those who gathered:

Thank you for being our life raft when it felt like we were so close to drowning.

TABLE OF CONTENTS

PREFACE

Ripples of deep loss and grief didn't shake my life for a remarkably long time. As I approached the end of my twenties, I had never experienced the death of a close relative—all four of my grandparents were even still alive.

That changed when I was 12 weeks pregnant with my first daughter. The pregnancy started as smoothly as I understood pregnancies to go: some nausea, surprising aversions (meat!) and overwhelming cravings (citrus!), but all normal and necessary steps when growing a human.

Everything was perfect at my eight-week ultrasound, so I entered my routine 12-week ultrasound expecting the same. It was far from routine and far from perfect.

The sonographer identified some abnormalities, namely large fluid pockets in the baby's heart and lungs known as *hydrops*, and a *cystic hygroma* that appeared like a huge space helmet around the baby's head. My baby girl Maisy was shortly thereafter diagnosed with *Turner Syndrome*, a genetic condition that impacts the endocrine system.

I'm a top-notch catastrophizer when I play the game of "what-ifs." When I first became pregnant, I started thinking, *What if my baby has spina bifida or one of those scary rare diseases?* Everyone said to me, "Don't worry, I'm sure it will all be fine."

But sometimes, the "what-ifs" become reality.

Based on the *Turner Syndrome* diagnosis and Maisy's symptoms, doctors anticipated her to have virtually no chance of survival. My husband, Kevin, and I went to the doctor twice a week for heartbeat checks, waiting for the "inevitable" day when the fluid we saw on the ultrasound would overcome her heart and lungs. It was every parent's nightmare.

Fast-forward six gut-wrenching weeks. We were at an appointment with our high-risk obstetrician. She said she nearly fell out of her chair at what she saw on this ultrasound compared to the previous ones. The *hydrops* had miraculously resolved, and the *hygroma* was waning—Maisy might actually make it.

The rest of my pregnancy was full of restrictions, constant evaluation and many unknowns. After nearly 40 hours of induced labor, Maisy was born via C-section at 37 weeks and immediately transported to the Cardiac ICU. She had open-heart surgery at six days old and remained in the hospital for a month of recovery.

Despite the rocky start, Maisy is doing amazingly well today. She has encountered plenty of challenges: feeding difficulties, countless ear infections, frequent specialist visits and growth hormone injections, to name a few. And we grieve for some of the difficulties to come, like the fact she won't be able to conceive biological children of her own. But even though the "what-if" of a rare disease became reality for our family, everything turned out better than we could have imagined.

Two years after Maisy was born, we got pregnant with our second daughter, Hope. We were overjoyed. I remember saying to my friends, "Well, there's no way this is going to be worse or more stressful than my pregnancy with Maisy!"

Boy, was I wrong.

At my 12-week ultrasound, in the same doctor's office, with the same sonographer, a different anomaly was detected: This time, it was *alobar holoprosencephaly* (HPE for short), a brain development condition that occurs at weeks two or three of pregnancy. It meant that Hope's brain did not successfully divide into two hemispheres. While this condition is known to be as common as one in 200 pregnancies, it typically leads to early-term miscarriage, which is what we were told to expect.[1]

If Hope did make it through early pregnancy and survive delivery, doctors predicted she would live for less than 24 hours and would need extreme medical intervention to support breathing, any kind of feeding and all life function beyond her heart beating.

Woof. Even I hadn't catastrophized a "what-if" scenario that extreme.

Kevin and I underwent extensive genetic testing and learned that both Maisy's and Hope's conditions were completely random and non-hereditary…meaning, this was just a "lightning strikes twice" scenario.

As with Maisy, we prayed and hoped for a miracle,

but no matter what, we were committed to seeing Hope's pregnancy through and celebrating her life—however long or short it might be.

Hope was born on October 7, 2023, at 36 weeks, after a 43-hour labor. For the last 24 hours of that labor, I didn't feel her move, and I braced for the worst. Pushing was the easy part: It took less than 10 minutes to usher her four-pound body into the world. I'll never forget the sound of her first cry as she emerged. Kevin and I burst into tears of shock and joy—we got to meet our daughter alive.

After confirming her diagnosis in the hospital and hearing her life would be vegetative at best, extremely painful at worst, we took her home on hospice care. We wanted to cherish every moment with her and surround her with the love of friends and family.

Hope died peacefully on October 21, 2023, 14 days later. She completed her short sprint of a life and brought us so much joy and beauty in the process. It was heart-wrenching for all of us, and explaining death to two-year-old Maisy was salt in the wound.

Throughout both of these pregnancies—and particularly throughout the life and death of Hope—we were an open book, sharing our daily updates, lamentations and needs. And we received so much love and support from our community of family, friends, caregivers and coworkers.

This book is the culmination of the lessons I've learned about how to invite others into the grieving process—and how to show up for families, friends, workmates, neighbors, acquaintances or strangers when the worst of their "what-ifs" come to fruition.

Life is short. Loss is hard.

Let's be in it together.

CHAPTER ONE

Grocery Store Encounters

As I sit down to coalesce my thoughts and experiences about grief, I find myself on a little grey sofa in my living room. The same sofa where my beloved daughter, Hope, died in my arms just over four months ago. When Hope was born, the leaves on the trees were still green. And by the time she passed, just two weeks later, the leaves had transformed to red, fallen and withered on the ground. The week of her funeral, we had our first snow.

The leaves haven't grown back yet, but early buds are forming, and I know new life will come. Life and death. Death and life. Death surrounds us every day—from leaves on trees, to pets leaving us, to long lives lived, to terminal diagnoses, to shocking tragedies. It's around us on the news, on our feeds and in our communities. But if death is so commonplace, why is it so difficult to talk about?

Imagine if you and I met at the grocery store, as I met many a well-wisher when I was pregnant with Hope. Pleasant strangers would offer me congratulations, and I would politely smile and thank them.

Then came the waterfall of typical prenatal questions.

"Aw, boy or girl?"

"Girl."

"When's she due?"

"Early November."

"Have you picked out a name?"

"Yes, Hope."

"What a nice name. Is there any reason behind that?"

Sigh. "Yes, because she has a terminal brain condition called *alobar holoprosencephaly* that we've known about since our 12-week ultrasound. We've had a litany of tests performed, and doctors agree that she will likely not live very long—probably just a few hours. We have hope that her short life won't be the end of her story or ours, so we thought it was a perfect name for her."

Big gasp. Hand covering mouth. Horrified expression. Stunned silence. "Oh…"

I mean, what would you—a well-meaning fellow grocery shopper—do if you accidentally wandered into that mess of a conversation?

One time, I got, "Wow. That's the saddest thing I've heard in a really long time."

Yeah, you're telling me.

Imagine living it and having this same conversation at least three times a day with every passerby, coworker, new acquaintance, neighbor. As it turns out, pregnancy can be fairly obvious and often invites comment, welcomed or not.

It's awkward for you. It's super awkward for me, because now I'm trying to tend to your grief in addition to my own. I also look like a psychopath for not emotionally reacting when I've just told you my unborn daughter is going to die soon. But that's only because I've practiced this three times today.

So what is the right thing to say in a situation like that? Or what is the wrong thing to say? And how can we know?

I'm writing this book for two groups of people:

1) People experiencing grief or loss (on any scale—it doesn't have to be death) who don't know how to articulate what they need or don't have the emotional capacity to coach others up on Grief 101; and

2) Family members, friends, colleagues, neighbors and acquaintances of those who are hurting, who genuinely want to offer help or encouragement but don't know where to begin.

The tricky thing is, everyone experiences different losses and everyone grieves differently. This book does not offer a one-size-fits-all method or a decoder ring for every personality type and situation. But it does offer a practical starting point to help you show up when it matters most.

I firmly believe it's essential to bring people into your grief. And if someone you know is hurting, it's better to say something than nothing at all (even if it feels awkward).

One caveat: It's better to say something *out of genuine care for another human being* than it is to say nothing at all.

Thanks for joining the journey.

CHAPTER TWO

Why Are We So Uncomfortable Talking About Grief?

NEWSFLASH: People have been disappointed, separated, pained and prone to die since the beginning of humanity.

So why is it such a shock to us today, particularly in American society?

With the strides the medical industry has taken during the last 50 years, death can seem surmountable. It has become the final frontier to conquer. We have so many methods to reverse aging, optimize health and defeat disease, making it a shock when we cannot "win" this battle.

Don't get me wrong, I'm incredibly thankful for these modern interventions (Maisy wouldn't be here without them!). But ultimately, *we will all meet death.*

My current plan is to die peacefully at age 90, of sound mind and body, while holding hands with Kevin, who conveniently dies at the same moment, à la *The Notebook*. This peaceful passage is to occur on a bright, sunny day as our kids and grandkids and great-grandkids huddle around us with love and hugs and Shipley Do-Nuts as they send us off to the Heavenly realm in perfect contentment and the recognition of lives well lived.

Odds are, that probably won't be the case.

Not long ago, our society interacted with the cycle of natural life and death on a daily basis. Just think about life on the farm: animals being born, procreating and dying. This was not an anomaly. It was expected.

Death still surrounds us today, but often in a distant or discordant way. Much of the death we encounter is filtered through the lens of a news broadcast or social media post. And it's all too often due to tragedy, not natural, honorable, inevitable circumstances.

Often in my mind, death equals trauma. But I don't think that was always the case.

A Brief History of Funerary Tradition

According to the Library of Congress, 40% of children in 1600s colonial America died before reaching adulthood.[2] Community members typically gathered for wakes to feast and drink with the mourning family.

The American funeral industry we recognize today was catalyzed by the American Civil War. Families were eager to bring the bodies of their loved ones home for burial and not leave them in enemy territory. Embalming was popularized for the general public following President Lincoln's assassination in 1865, when he was then carried on a two-week public procession by train from Washington, D.C. to his final resting place of Springfield, Illinois.[3]

In the early 1900s, funeral homes and private burials were increasingly common.[4] Public wakes decreased in popularity, particularly following the 1918 Spanish Flu outbreak, when the government eliminated public funeral gatherings and mandated burials within 24 hours to stifle the spread of infection.[5]

These changes led to the decline of community support and gathering around funerals. In some places, like my current home state of Colorado, human remains must be dispositioned (embalmed, buried, etc.) within 24 hours of death.[6] And while wakes (or viewings) still occur, they are likely much different than broad community gatherings of the past.

Expectations Around Loss

Based on the general clumsiness I've encountered when talking about death and loss, it's safe to say our muscles of dealing with grief as a community have atrophied in the United States.

I discovered just how much I didn't know about the norms of death and grief when I was planning Hope's funeral. There were so many decisions to make with very little context about how to make them.

The list easily overwhelms:

- Do you want an open casket?
- Who will be invited?
- Will there be refreshments?
- What should I wear?
- Will everyone invited to the ceremony also attend the burial?

Funerals are so common, so why does it often feel like we're starting from scratch? How do I know if a decision will have an enduring impact or if it's just another box to check?

If you Google "American funeral traditions," you're likely to find a bunch of listings from funeral homes talking about services and amenities—not necessarily helpful guidance on what you might expect. Does anyone have this figured out? My curiosity prompted me to explore global customs related to death.

One rich tradition I encountered in my research is the Jewish tradition of shiva, a period of seven days following the funeral of a loved one. Sheloshim is the period of 30 days from the day of the funeral.[7] For the first year following the funeral of a parent, grieving children are still in a period of mourning and recite the Mourner's Kaddish daily.[8] Each of these periods and other marked dates (anniversaries, etc.) require abstinence from certain activities, like celebratory events.

There are commonly understood expectations for each of these phases. In fact, shiva is a dedicated week-long period where community members bring food to the mourners and sit low to the ground to be with grievers in their time of loss.[9] It is a time of emotional and spiritual encouragement.

Wouldn't it be nice if people automatically knew to bring you food and flowers during a period of loss? And sat with you, often in silence, without you having to ask?

The Greek Orthodox tradition recognizes a series of planned Trisagion prayer services: immediately following a death; at the funeral before the coffin is lowered into the grave; three days following the death; nine days following the death; on the 40th day; and at the three-, six-, nine- and 12-month marks, then annually.[10]

Traditional Chinese culture recognizes a mourning period, called shǒusāng, of up to three years. In Confucian times, there were established rules and prohibitions around food, clothing and certain activities. Some ancient customs are still in practice today—like wearing specific colors or materials to represent a griever's relation to the deceased.[11]

Without trying to oversimplify global grief traditions, my general observation is that many societies offer more organized rituals than what I've witnessed in my corner of the United States.

Grief never confines itself to a timeline, process or ritual. There is no way to develop a formula or custom that will erase the sorrow that comes from deep loss, but it can help to establish some norms and expectations for our communities as we move through grief and invite others to join us.

We need to revisit our communal roots and bring people alongside us in our griefs and our joys. Life is meant to be lived in community. And the more vulnerable, the better.

Like It or Not, Here We Come

My friend Nadja is someone who prefers processing difficult things privately. She admits she doesn't like to reach out to others or detail the intimacies of her challenges and sorrows and scares. Nadja is from Bosnia, and she shared with me that in her culture, even if you are an internal processor, community will give you no choice but to be surrounded. When Nadja's grandfather passed away, the whole village gathered around her family and brought food. Even though Nadja says she might not have invited them if it were up to her, it was comforting that people showed up anyway to honor her grandfather.

In countries like the U.S. where grieving customs might not be so communal, it's an unexpected gift when people choose to surround and support you in your time of need.

Be an Erin

Case in point: my dear coworker Erin. Erin and I rarely worked directly together, but we became friends over two years of bumping into each other in the restroom down the hall from our respective offices.

Over time, we learned about each other's backgrounds and families and discovered we share the same alma mater. I told her the news of Hope's diagnosis, and she was one of those people who came out of the woodwork to support our family. We had a lot of family members and friends we knew we could count on through this journey, but it was such a sweet surprise to have someone we didn't know well enter into our sorrows with us.

After Hope passed, Erin got my personal phone number from another workmate (with permission), reached out to me and brought our family a wonderful homemade dinner, including the best chocolate chip cookies I've ever tasted. She also brought Maisy a doll and gifted me a spa package—amazing! But the best part of all was that she joined us for three hours as we savored the dinner she had prepared. She asked questions about our family's journey, listened as we shared and really cared to know how we were doing. We laughed and we cried. Together. After returning to work, I ran into Erin and thanked her for being so intentional during our time of need.

She told me she was relieved it had been helpful, that she really wanted to help but she didn't know where to start. She admitted, "I even Googled it! What do you do when someone loses a baby?"

Her unexpected kindness (especially because we had previously been just casual associates and bathroom buddies) was such an overwhelmingly positive surprise.

And it had a huge impact on me. It impacted her as well. Erin told me that a member of her team recently experienced a miscarriage and that he was taking some time off to grieve with his wife. She said she texted him to check in but debated saying anything when he returned to the office for fear it would be awkward or too painful.

And she said to me, "I wasn't going to say anything. But then I thought about what you said…how it's better to say something, even if it feels awkward, than to just ignore it and move on like nothing happened."

So she did it! She said something. She told me it was

a brief exchange—kind of awkward—but she thinks it was appreciated.

Perhaps you're sitting on the other side of this. Maybe your family and friends don't ever mention the loss of your child. Maybe you didn't want to tell them. Maybe they didn't know how to listen. Maybe they said something silly like, "It will be okay. Everything happens for a reason!" Maybe the would-be due date sails by with no cards, no hugs, no cookies. Only silence. If that's you, I'm so sorry for your loss.

Saying something isn't about checking a box. And it's definitely not about probing for gossip, or making yourself feel better because you "reached out." In fact, it's not about you at all. It's about expressing genuine care and empathy for those who are in the pits.

I wish we could all have people like Erin in our lives. People who go the extra mile to be there with us. It doesn't always have to cost something either—a hug, a text, a card. You might never know how much that could lift someone's spirit.

And even more than wanting to have more Erins in my life, I hope to become more like Erin. To be courageous. To overcome situational discomfort and truly be there for people, even if I only know them from the office bathroom.

But where do we begin?

CHAPTER THREE

The Invitation

How do we know if people are hurting and need help? And how do we magically summon people like Erin into our lives when we are the ones who need support?

It starts with an invitation to openness and vulnerability.

Listen, we are all humans. This means we have probably all experienced disappointment in relationships, pain caused by others and the discomfort that comes from unrequited vulnerability. It can become a protective mechanism—often learned in childhood—to suppress our emotions. Just take Elsa from *Frozen* as an example of what can go wrong when you try to hide your pain, only to cause a massive explosion of ice.

It takes tremendous courage to share the real stuff—the ups and downs of daily life. And the things inside that cause us fear and pain or excitement and joy. But at the end of the day, who we are is worth sharing.

Granted, there might be an appropriate time and setting for certain depths of sharing. And it's always wise to evaluate your audience and set appropriate boundaries for conversations (more on that in Chapter Four). But it's okay to take a risk—to throw out an invitation and see how others respond.

I've spent the majority of my career at a Fortune 100 company, and even among the glossy floors and dispassionate cubicles of Corporate America, I've found that an appropriate level of vulnerability is greatly appreciated and very often reciprocated.

Some of my bosses and colleagues have been personable, yet highly impersonal. Others have been very personal, but not always so personable. I find the balance of both *personal* and *personable* so refreshing. And when you bring your whole self to work, you usually end up doing your best work. Win. Win. Win.

I've found the same to be true in my personal life. I spent 12 years of my childhood in Southeast Asia, primarily in Singapore. Right before my sophomore year of high school, my dad accepted a new job that landed us in Orlando, Florida.

Boy, was that tough. Even though I was an American citizen by birth, I felt no real connection to American culture. I didn't know what to wear, how to do my hair or how to operate in a 5,000-person public high school after coming from a private Christian school with 200 students.

On my first day of school, I awkwardly forced my way into a lunch group, which only narrowly beat out the alternative of eating alone in the bathroom. It was painfully lonely. All the extracurriculars I'd excelled at in a small school environment were stripped away as I plunged into the reality of the big Florida public school pond.

I put myself out there time and again, and I felt rejected and alone, time and again. Thankfully, over time, I got involved in new extracurriculars (hello, water polo), met new friends and cultivated new skills. After a year of intense immersion, I had even found myself a fairly stable lunch group.

That big move as a 15-year-old was pretty bleak, but it made my transition to a large public university with about 50,000 students a piece of cake. I knew how to be new and start building relationships wherever I went. Now in my thirties, that skill has continued to serve me well as I've navigated various cross-country moves and job transitions.

The secret? Invite people into your life. And invite yourself into their lives and see who sticks.

It's hard to keep putting yourself out there and being vulnerable again and again. I've formed deep relationships and sometimes kissed them goodbye. I've put hope and time into new friend groups that all too often didn't pan out.

On several occasions, I've gone all in sharing my stories, hopes and dreams, only to wake up to what I call a vulnerability hangover: that gut punch you feel when you realize you've hopefully cannonballed into the waters of friendship while your new buddy was only planning to dip a toe. You went skinny dipping. She sat on the edge of the hot tub. It can feel shameful and might even lead you to believe a lie that you are not worth knowing. Reject the lie, learn from this and keep putting yourself out there. It can be lonely and painful, but in my experience, it's really the only way to survive. And ultimately, to thrive.

I'm ever the extrovert, so people truly are key to my surviving and thriving, but regardless of temperament, it's a foundational part of humanity to build friendships and relationships that provide you a space to be vulnerable. That is healthy and good in the best of times—and essential in the worst of times.

Another Transition

In early 2022, our little family of three moved from the central Denver area to a suburb farther from the city. I was hungry for new relationships as our former community had disintegrated and dramatically changed as a product of COVID-19. Aside from one amazing cousin, we don't have any family in the state, so we rely on our network of friends, neighbors and colleagues a lot.

Church is a big part of our lives and where we've found the majority of our close relationships in the past. In late summer, our new neighbors invited us to their church, and it was an immediate fit. We had "tried on" several other churches and were so thankful to find a landing spot. We quickly got involved in weekly men's and women's groups and found friends in similar life stages.

Note: This book is not focused on faith and grief, but I can't help but acknowledge it here, since my faith in Jesus—His death and resurrection and promise of eternal life—is my foundation and my ultimate anchor in the darkest days. Even though it didn't always feel like it, I know God was with us through our trials because of how He paired us with this particular church community, connected us to other families who have lost children and gave us some of the best friendships of our lives in the span of mere months.

Just like every other time I started fresh, I began with an invitation to vulnerability. But this time, it was easy, like I had never experienced before, and I am forever thankful we had this community around us during Hope's life and death. When you are walking through life's toughest moments, I hope you find community like this, or that it finds you.

No matter where you find it, the key is authentic connection, which starts with an invitation into life: the good, the bad, the ugly.

Now let's get to the heart of it: As a community member in need, how can you ask for help? And as a community member who wants to help, how can you show up when it matters most?

CHAPTER FOUR

Where Do I Begin?

It can be scary to admit the need for help. Or even scarier, to ask for it. But it's okay to not be okay, to need others, to be open with those around you and to receive their support. Here are some tips for when you are the one who is experiencing grief or loss.

No Comparing

It never helps to compare griefs.

And once again for the folks in the back: It *never* helps.

Let's say you just lost your dad and your teammate just lost their dog. You are both sad and spending time and money to say your final goodbyes and prepare for burials.

You are heartbroken because this was not only your father, but your handyman, tax consultant, lifelong coach and favorite shoulder to cry on.

Maybe you're the one who just lost your dog, and you are really broken up about it because this dog was your best friend and faithful companion in your solo apartment.

Or maybe, you're the person who lost your dad two years ago and then lost your dog right after your break-up the same week your car broke down, and the grief from losing your dog really reminds you of the grief from losing your dad, and now all these extra stressful things are also going wrong, and you're spiraling into a new level of explosive emotion that others might not realize is deeper than "just" the loss of a pet. So, *excuse me* if I'm having a public meltdown at the office refrigerator, Janet!

Objectively, losing a parent and losing a dog could be considered different "tiers" of loss, but loss doesn't play by rules. And there's no such thing as "objective" when it comes to grief.

Perhaps you're dealing with some other kind of loss—property damage, identity theft, infertility, double mastectomy after a breast cancer diagnosis, career disruption, broken relationship, car accident, mental overload, arguments with your partner…you name it. It's all icky, and it's not to be compared.

In the end, no one ever really "wins" the game of grief comparison.

No Minimizing

I sometimes find myself thinking, *Well, at least I didn't lose my husband,* or *At least I'm not facing genocide,* or *At least I still have food on the table.*

Yes, all of those things are true, and I encourage you to use those types of thoughts to fuel genuine gratitude and perspective…but not to minimize the legitimate pain you are in.

Get the Help You Need

I'm glad you are reading this book! That means you are seeking resources or at least curious enough to take a peek.

Here are some of the resources that helped me when I was pregnant with Hope—and still help, many moons later.

Therapy: Kevin and I started seeing a counselor together when we first received Hope's diagnosis. She helped us so much in the process of preparing for Hope. And through the course of many months, she's helped us with many other aspects of our marriage.

Medication: After Maisy was born, three different doctors approached me about medication for anxiety. Eventually, I thought, *Well, if all of these people are bringing this up independently, maybe I should consider it.* I was nervous it would change who I was or make me numb. It didn't. As Kevin puts it, the medication helps me turn down the background rave music in my head so I can increase focus on the situation at hand. Everyone has a different experience, but I'm so grateful I listened to those doctors. I have continued to get input from my psychiatrist to help adjust my medications as needed through the seasons.

Chiropractic/Massage Therapy: I have an amazing massage therapist and a chiropractor who is also a massage therapist (did I mention I love massages?) that I see about once a month to help me work through the pain and tension my physical body is holding. They work wonders.

Coworkers: I was very open with my colleagues and boss about my pregnancies and difficulties. They were so supportive while I was still at work and graciously took over my responsibilities while I was on leave.

Friends: Back to community. My truest friends understand when I just need to sit with them, or when Kevin and I need a break from Maisy so we can get some alone time, or when I ask them to visit Hope's grave with me. Or when I'm ready to kick back and laugh and not think about hard times.

Family: Even though our families live far away, they all made every effort to be with us for Hope's brief life and funeral. And they continue to honor her memory. As we've lost our daughter, they've lost their granddaughter, niece, cousin. Christmas came just two months after Hope died, and my mom set a little figurine on the mantle to represent Hope, as well as a Hershey's Kiss to symbolize my grandmother, who also passed away in 2023. This touch was present, but not central. Honoring without distracting. It was a sweet way to remember and include our beloved family members who wouldn't be joining that year's festivities.

Others Who Have a Shared Experience: It can be comforting to talk to others who have walked, or are walking, a similar path. Read more about this in Chapter Six.

I recognize there's privilege inherent in each of these categories. Access to resources, money to pay for massages, a job that granted me a leave of absence. Whatever your situation, hopefully something on this list resonates with you.

Set Boundaries

It's okay to ask people you trust for things you need—and to tell them graciously what is not helpful at this time. And if someone offers to help, assume they mean it.

You will find some people naturally draw closer to you during times of loss while others bolt in the opposite direction. You have the freedom to set boundaries—to invite closer the ones who are encouraging and to set limits on those who say silly or hurtful things or those who say nothing at all.

When dealing with all of the above responses, be

gracious. Loss is complicated and hits us all in different ways. And it's a time when we often feel more sensitive to pretty much everything. If you're in relationship with humans, you will be surrounded by messy people, most of whom have positive intentions and are trying to say and do the right thing but simply might not know how.

Here are several reactions you might encounter:

Support: Some people—like Erin!—want to come alongside you and support you. Their presence is generally encouraging and helpful to you. It can occasionally be overbearing, but it's typically backed by good intentions.

Silence:

- **Present Silence**: Sometimes, silence is sacred and comforting. A loved one's presence is more powerful than any words.
- **Uncomfortable Silence**: People might not say anything because they feel awkward and don't want to cause you pain by bringing up a stinging memory. Although, it's not like you're not already thinking about it anyway.

- **Toxic Silence**: Sometimes, silence looks like distance or anger. A strongly negative emotional response usually says less about your loss and more about the emotional health of the person reacting, likely driven by some type of grief, insecurity, remorse or pain in their own life.

Intentional Hurt: If people are saying things to intentionally harm you, those are not the people you want to be surrounded by—in bad times or in good times. Set a boundary.

Unintentional Hurt: This can look a million different ways, from thoughtless comments to comparisons to "at least…" statements. My rule about unintentional hurt is this: The closer the person is to you who made a thoughtless statement, the more likely it is to hurt, and the more important it is to address or confront. The less personal the relationship, the less likely a thoughtless comment is to hurt and the less important it is to address.

The diagram below is based on my interactions during Hope's life and death. It illustrates the four categories above and offers suggestions of who to protect against (see the hard lines to indicate firm boundaries) and who to bring closer (the dotted lines).

A Note on Confrontation

When I was pregnant with Hope, several acquaintances asked me directly, “Couldn’t you just have an abortion?” The answer, in Colorado at least, was yes.

This question always surprised me because it was so blunt. But whether it was because I wasn’t particularly close to the individual asking, or I could tell they asked the question out of well-meaning curiosity, the question didn't typically offend me.

This question gave me an opportunity to share my perspective and why Kevin and I made the choices we did. And I made it clear we had no regrets, even though it was a hard path.

That said, if someone I considered to be an extremely close friend were to ask this same question, I might have taken offense at their brazen tone. If it stuck with me in a way that impacted our friendship, I would press myself to an ultimatum:

> **Choice A – Let Sleeping Dogs Lie**: Pull back from this friend during this season to protect my extra-sensitive self in this time. It's not worth expending energy right now to confront this person, and long-term, I don't think this will be a barrier to our friendship.

> **Choice B – Confrontation**: I am really counting on this person to be with me through this season of loss, and that comment irked me because it left me feeling like they don't know or understand me. They probably didn't mean it to be offensive or brash, but it hurt my feelings in a way

that impacts my ability to trust and be open with them. Because of that, it's worth investing the time and energy—even when those are very scarce resources during this season—to let them know and try to move past this. If they don't respond well, then they are not someone I can count on to be a member of my innermost circle in this time of need.

Once that is decided, if I were to go with Choice B (Confrontation), the conversation might go like this:

> *"Hey, the other day when we were talking, I was caught off guard by something you said. I am assuming you didn't mean it to be hurtful. Your friendship means a lot to me, and it's worth it to me to bring this up and talk about it so we can move forward. It wasn't so much the nature of the question that bothered me but how you presented it, which made me feel like you don't understand my approach or history. Maybe next time you could try something like, 'I imagine you have had to make some tough decisions on this journey, including whether or not you wanted to continue the pregnancy. What was that like for you?' Again, it's because I value our friendship so much that I wanted to address this with you. What do you think?"*

Every time I've had this conversation within a healthy, secure relationship, the reaction has always been genuine remorse—followed by an invitation to move through the hurtful moment and into a deeper relationship.

In unhealthy or insecure relationships, I have experienced people lashing out, deflecting and saying things like, "So, I guess I should just stop trying to ask you questions then, huh?"

This type of response immediately turns the focus away from your feedback and centers it on the respondent, exposing their insecurity and immaturity. This type of self-focused response is a good indicator you might want to back away from this particular friend during this season.

Accept Help

In the next chapter, I encourage supporters to offer specific examples of how to help, rather than a general statement of "Let me know if there's anything I can do to help!"

And if nothing comes to mind, just say, "I can't think of anything I need right now, but thanks so much for asking! If you want, you could check in next week and see if anything pops up between now and then. Thank you!"

Share Updates

Throughout my pregnancies with Maisy and Hope, I maintained a blog where I could post updates for family members and friends. It was cathartic to have a place to pour out my thoughts and updates. But it became much more than a diary—it was a great portal to streamline communication when things were at their most overwhelming. When friends, neighbors or teammates texted me to ask for updates, I would often send the link to my blog and say something like, "Thanks so much for checking in. The best way to get the latest is to follow my posts. Here's the link…"

I'm already pretty bad about texting people back in a timely manner, and adding postpartum recovery and extreme stress to the mix did not foster responsiveness. I had an inner circle of about five people who got the longer, more personal text updates on a daily basis…but for everyone else, the website was a great way to stay connected without expending a lot of precious time and emotional energy.

Be Patient

Finally, the best advice I can give: Be patient with yourself, with others, with your circumstances, with your children and with your partner. You and those grieving alongside you will respond to things very differently. You will likely want and need very different things. You will probably get on each other's nerves without even realizing why…until one of you suddenly bursts into tears and you realize, *oh yeah, it's about our grief again*.

Our incredible therapist, Sue, gave Kevin and me some great advice about dwelling on grief. She told us to think about grief as a big object. I think of a cloud hanging in an empty room.

The cloud is always there, but you don't always have to spend hours in the room visiting it.

Some days, you might just need to open the door, peek in and then walk away.

Some days, you might sit with it for hours and let it enshroud you.

Some days, you might not even be ready to open the door. And that's okay.

Please be patient and very gentle with yourself.

CHAPTER FIVE

Let Me Know How I Can Help

If you picked up this book because you are going to a funeral or you are wanting to learn more about how to help someone who is in a time of emotional distress, this is it! This is the chapter especially for you.

Start by reviewing the previous chapter. It's designed for those who are in the pit of despair themselves, and it might introduce a new perspective or fresh empathy as you're seeking to support someone in need.

An important thing to remember: Everyone grieves differently. There is no formula. Some friends might be waiting for you to reach out. Others might appreciate a slow-and-steady approach. Some might not want to share anything with you at all. That said, here are a few general guidelines on how to approach those who are experiencing loss.

Start with Empathy

Even if the loss someone else describes doesn't seem like it "should" be a huge deal—or certainly doesn't compare to the level of grief you've experienced, there's no need to share that with them at this time, or ever.

Be a listener, a validator, a shoulder to lean on. And if you have experienced deep grief, be the kind of friend you wish you'd had during that season.

Don't Try To Fix It

Your job is just to be there. To bring food if they need food. To provide childcare if they need childcare. To take care of the cat if the cat needs care. To be silent if they need silence. To laugh if they need laughter. Your job is not to re-diagnose the issue.

By the time Hope was born, I was pretty unsurprised—and unaffected—by insensitive comments. I'd heard them all. And for the most part, I was able to respond with grace and empathy when people said something that was less than ideal. But it would drive me nuts when people would add their own diagnosis or conjecture to the issue.

Example A

Pointing to my belly: "Congrats!"

"Thank you," I say, trying to manage expectations. "She has a terminal diagnosis, and doctors don't think she'll live very long."

"Oh no! That's awful! I'm sure you'll have more time with her than you think."

Oh shoot, would more time mean prolonged suffering for her? I haven't thought through this enough. And that's another thing to worry about.

I don't even know what to say to that, so I say, "We are looking forward to meeting her, and we will see how it all goes."

Example B

Pointing to my belly: "Congrats!"

"Thank you," once again tempering expectations. "She has a terminal diagnosis, and doctors don't think she'll live very long."

Then comes the absolute worst non sequitur: "Aww, but you guys are such a good family. I'm sure everything will be okay."

Many of the well-meaning people in my life (typically people I didn't interact with very frequently—neighbors, fellow gym-goers, casual work friends, etc.) sought to downplay the severity of the bad news I shared with them. I don't think it was ever malicious or intentional. It's a knee-jerk response to bad news infused with our modern societal need to "fix it."

The "good people" one, in particular, never made sense to me…as if being a nice person means you won't experience hardship. Sometimes I would say things like, "You know, while of course we would love a miracle and believe that can happen, we don't expect the circumstances to change. It's absolutely devastating, but we are holding on tight as a family."

These types of interactions often left me feeling overlooked rather than comforted. The same applied to "Everything happens for a reason," "God's got a plan," "This will make you stronger," "God doesn't give things we can't handle, so you must be able to handle it," and other unhelpful comments along these lines. While these platitudes might be true, I was aggravated to the core when that was a well-wisher's first response.

Bottom line: Please don't attempt to put the "it will all be okay" bandage on the situation. It's much better to say something like, "I'm so sorry you are going through this. Is it okay if I give you a hug?"

Sometimes, the best thing might be a text to let someone know you're there for them: "Sending you lots of love. This sucks, and I'm sorry it's happening to you."

Offer Help You Are Willing to Cheerfully Give

It's a great instinct to offer someone help when they are in need. Many of us, myself included, have said things like, "Do you need anything?" or "Let me know how I can help!"

As someone who has needed lots of help in different seasons, I find I never know what to say to that offer. Either I don't know what I actually need, or there's something that would be a huge help, but I'm afraid it would inconvenience a friend too much.

Here are some examples of what someone overwhelmed by grief might ask for or need:

> *Would you mind picking my kids up from school this afternoon?*

> *I have so many new appointments on the calendar, and I'm concerned about being late or insufficiently prepared for the work meeting on Thursday. Would you mind taking the lead this week?*

> *I ran out of contact solution. Would you mind grabbing me some while you're at the store this afternoon?*

❝ *Can you pick my relative up from the airport?*

❝ *I miss you. Do you think you could plan a visit and stay with us while we sort through this? It would be so helpful to have you here to help with meals, dishes, laundry, bedtime, etc.*

❝ *I'd love it if you could just come over one day next week for some wine and a movie. Would you be up for that?*

On the other side of that coin, as someone who is offering support, try offering up some very specific and practical suggestions:

❝ *I'm going to the store tomorrow. Can I grab you any snacks or medicines or anything while I'm there?*

❝ *Would it be helpful to have people drop off meals? I would love to set up a meal train for you.*

❝ *I will be in your neck of the woods on Tuesday after running to Panera. I'll plan to get an assortment of sandwiches/soups/salads and drop them off at your front door around 6 p.m. If you have any restrictions/preferences (or have other plans tomorrow), let me know and I'll try a different day!*

❝ *Can I watch your kid(s) for a few hours next Thursday to give you some reprieve?*

❝ *Do you need a ride to your appointment? Or would you just like some company? I'd love to be there for you.*

❝ *Would you like me to feed or walk your dog while you're at the hospital today?*

Offer things you are willing to give to the person in need. And if they take you up on it, that's fantastic! They are trusting you and letting you in. Deliver on your offer to help.

And if you drop off food (which I always loved), please use disposable containers so washing, labeling and returning Tupperware containers is not added to your grieving friend's to-do list.

Be Okay with Delayed Responses and Rejected or Deferred Offers

Following Hope's diagnosis, we were fortunate to have friends and family members reach out and offer help. This was absolutely appropriate and appreciated, but it soon became overwhelming. My calendar—already packed with a two-year-old, a full-time job, social commitments and morning sickness—was now overflowing with additional appointments (doctors, specialists, grief therapy, etc.).

I cannot tell you how much I appreciated people reaching out after my appointments to gather updates. And how much it meant when people delivered meals in those early days. And how much I wanted to have people around me in that scary time.

It meant so much to me that people went out of their way to check in. Some even invited me out to coffee or lunch to catch up. Of course I wanted to connect with these thoughtful people, but I was just so exhausted and overwhelmed. Instead of appreciating this kind gesture, I often felt guilty that I didn't have—or make more time—to connect with well-wishers.

One of Kevin's teammates, Adam, intuited this. He asked Kevin if he wanted to meet up for happy hour. Less than 30 minutes later, he texted again and said, "So, I just realized that in trying to do something nice for you, I asked for your time—*and you probably don't have a lot of that to spare right now*...No need to schedule anything now, and you're always welcome to take me up on that offer when it works for you!"

Kevin and I were both blown away by the self-awareness and wisdom displayed by this astute gentleman in his twenties. We both felt so seen by this gesture. There was no guilt to be had for saying "No," or "Maybe in six weeks when things settle down a bit." What a gift.

No, You Don't Know How They Feel

If you read Chapter Four, you'll note my caution to those grieving not to compare, and I encourage you to heed it as well. No one wins the comparison game when it comes to "worse loss" or "most grief." So, let's stop playing it.

Along the lines of comparison, even if you have been through something similar, please don't start with "I know how you feel…I remember when my brother went through this..."

You likely don't know *exactly* how they feel.

Consider this: After losing a loved one who has experienced prolonged pain or suffering, I've heard friends share their greatest emotion was "relief." But imagine saying to someone, "Wow, you must be so relieved" if they are *not* experiencing that emotion. What if they respond with, "*Relieved*? Why would I be *relieved* that my mother has died?" Yikes!

Unchecked assumptions can quickly lead to indelicate comments.

Conversely, imagine saying, “Wow, you must be so heartbroken,” when their first thought was relief. Now they’re left with guilt in addition to relief and likely also heartbreak. Much pain could be avoided if we asked, rather than told, someone how they feel.

If you have relevant experience, it might come in handy. Or it might not. Always keep the focus on your friend, not your personal story. Recognize that no two circumstances, diagnoses or relationships are identical.

If you genuinely think your experience might help, here’s a way to frame it: “I’m so sorry you’re going through this. I am here for you. I’m not sure if we talked about this, but my brother received that same diagnosis two years ago. It might be too much to talk through now, but if you’re ever interested in hearing about his journey with this disease, I’d be happy to connect with you if that feels helpful.”

If it doesn’t feel helpful to them right now and they decline your offer, don’t take offense!

Remove "At Least" From Your Vocabulary

This is *never* helpful to a person who is experiencing loss.

Oh, how the floodgates of "at least" opened after Hope's birth and death.

⊗ *Well, at least she was born alive.*

⊗ *At least you didn't have to have a C-section this time.*

⊗ *At least you got two weeks with her.*

I'm so thankful that Hope was born alive, that the birth experience was much less stressful than I had feared, and yes, what a blessing that I got to spend an amazing two weeks with her. I am very grateful for those things.

But the "at least" comments only ever made me feel smaller.

Oh yes, *at least* I got two weeks with her…*who the heck decided that was enough time to have with my baby before she died?*

Here are some alternatives that made me feel much better:

> *I am so glad you got to meet her alive! I know that was something you really hoped would happen.*

> *What was the delivery like for you? I can't imagine all the emotions that must have been swirling.*

> *I'm so sorry her time on Earth was so short. It was clear you all loved her so much.*

All of these statements lead with empathy and allow for space and open-endedness. They do not presume a certain emotion or reaction. As someone who likes to verbally process, these types of statements are inviting me into deeper conversation, should I choose to accept it. But even if I don't want to talk about it right now, these are comments that acknowledge my loss and make me feel seen.

Say Something

What's worse than saying something awkward? Saying nothing at all. I took three months of leave from work when Hope was born—some maternity leave and some bereavement/mental health leave. I'm so thankful I had a job with benefits that allowed me to take that time. It was absolutely restorative and essential to regaining my physical, emotional and mental health before re-entering the workforce.

Throughout my pregnancy, I was very transparent about Hope's prognosis, especially with the usual suspects at work (boss, team, office neighbors, bathroom buddies, etc.). The initial conversations were a bit awkward and sometimes painful, but I wanted the people around me to know so that I wouldn't return from maternity leave to a bunch of questions like, "How is your baby?" only to have to break the news.

When Hope passed, I had my manager send an email with our family photo and an update to about 75 associates. This also included an invitation to her memorial service.

By the time I returned to work on the second day of January, I had gotten really good at responding to different sentiments about the loss of Hope…even the "at least" comments. Whether people were outstandingly perceptive, overflowing with empathy or shocked into uncomfortable mumbles, I could take it in stride and respond appropriately. So, what happened when I returned to work completely shocked me.

The default response was to say nothing. Absolutely nothing. Not even, "I'm sorry for your loss."

The silence became a playground where my insecurities ran free. *Did they not get that announcement email? Did they forget? Do they just not care?*

A few people looked at me with sad eyes, followed by a question like, "So, how are you…doing?" I interpreted this as, "You lived through something hard, and I care about your well-being, but I don't know how to invite such a heavy topic into our office small talk, so I'll let you decide if you want to tell me more." Which made it easy to respond, "I'm doing fine! How about you?" rather than to share what was really on my mind.

To be fair, it wasn't everyone. Some coworkers had come to Hope's funeral. Some had texted me throughout leave and stayed in touch. You've already heard about Erin, who was the model of support.

But the default to silence really caught me off guard. I came to realize that even when I intentionally mentioned Hope in conversation, people shied away from asking questions or even saying her name.

I was ready for any flavor of comment, no matter how thoughtful or senseless, but I was not ready for silence.

I thought, *People are so uncomfortable about this topic! They don't know what to say. They don't want to make me cry.*

And that's really what made me start thinking about this book.

Kevin returned to work the same day and received the same avoidant response. When I told him about my shock and the feeling of hurt that came from not having this great loss acknowledged, he told me that I shouldn't judge others for their responses, and that he certainly didn't want people talking to him about grief all day.

Again, everyone deals with things differently, and there's no right way. I did ask Kevin if he would have been offended if someone said something like, "I'm sorry for your loss," or, "Thanks for sending those family photos."

The answer was no, he would not have been offended. And now, months later, he does like to talk about Hope and feels known when people ask about her.

By saying something, you risk momentary discomfort…but by saying nothing, you might risk an entire relationship.

Be brave like Erin. Choose to say something real. Be curious.

Ask Questions

There are a few people I can always count on to ask the real, true questions. I'm not always in the mood or place to answer them, but I appreciate them all the same.

If you're not sure what to say or what to ask, here are some ideas:

- *I'm so glad you're back in the office. I'd love to hear more about what you went through. Are you up for talking about it?*
- *What was that like for you?*
- *What decisions do you have to make next?*
- *Is there anything I can do (at work, home, school, etc.) to lighten your load this week?*
- *What feels heavy this week?*
- *Did you learn anything new at your appointment?*

- *Do you want to talk about it?*

- *That sounds scary and stressful. How are you holding up?*

- *It's been a few months since X. How are you feeling today?*

- *It seems like you've had a lot on your mind recently. I just want to let you know I'm here for you. Would you like to talk about it?*

It means a lot to me when people use Hope's name. It reminds me that she's real, and that others acknowledge the pain of losing her is real, too.

Most people who have lost someone dear to them like to share memories of those they grieve. Here are some questions you might try:

- *I'm so sorry you lost your (parent, sibling, partner, friend—if possible, use their name). What was she like?*

- *What do you miss most about him?*

- *What holiday traditions did you share with your mom?*

- *What memory makes you laugh?*

- *When does grief hit you the most?*

CHAPTER SIX

The World's Worst Club

On the day of Hope's funeral, my friend Chelsea said to me, "Welcome to the world's worst club…the club for those who have lost a child." Chelsea's daughter, Lydia, died from an unexpected seizure when she was six years old. Unfathomable.

We're all subscribed to various "clubs" of shared experience—whether it's a Costco membership, a high school class year or a dismal one like the grieving parent club. Some of these subscriptions require self-enrollment, while others are not ones you'd ever choose for yourself.

As soon as you swipe that card, enroll in the new school or get handed a diagnosis—the world of shared experience groups for this particular club will avail itself to you, typically via social media.

When we found out Maisy had *Turner Syndrome*, I began the frantic pregnant-mom-with-now-confirmed-reason-to-freak-out search frenzy, which can be quite overwhelming. I also had friends coming out of the woodwork to offer up their friends of friends who "experienced something similar and would be happy to connect." I genuinely appreciated the outreach, but the number of new resources was so overwhelming, and I didn't know what would be helpful and what would not.

Over time, I developed a filter to narrow down the resources and connections I would pursue during my precious free time.

Resources and Connections I Found Helpful

Assigned Medical Professionals: My number one resource was my assigned care team: the doctors, specialists and genetic counselors who could explain my specific situation and answer my many questions.

Shared Diagnosis Buddies: When Kevin and I received Maisy's diagnosis, I was introduced to Lexie, who walked a similar road of *Turner Syndrome* scary-diagnosis-to-miraculous-delivery with her daughter. She is about two years ahead of me on this journey. The first time I called her on the phone, we both blubbered as we shared our stories, and it was so comforting to hear from someone who really did know what it was like to get this kind of news and diagnosis.

During Maisy's first two years, I asked Lexie questions like: "What groups have you found helpful?" "Any tips on how to use a G-tube?" "Ah! Remind me again what I do when the G-tube button falls out?" "Our first time giving the growth hormone shot was terrible and all three of us are crying…Is this normal? Will it get better?"

It's been years since that initial conversation, and we have built a great relationship over time. She is someone who uniquely understands the challenges that come from parenting a medically complex child and knows the ins-and-outs of *Turner Syndrome* lingo. While Lexie's daughter and Maisy have vastly different nuances within their spectrum of care and diagnoses, it's a beautiful thing to share common ground.

Non-Profits Specific to My Situation: When I learned of Maisy's diagnosis, I was connected with the non-profit String of Pearls, a perinatal hospice organization designed to support families who have received terminal prenatal diagnoses and choose to continue the pregnancy.

String of Pearls was founded by an angel on Earth, Laura Huene, who formed this organization after her daughter Pearl passed away from a terminal disease a few short hours after birth.

From the get-go, String of Pearls sent us gifts like heartbeat-recording stuffed animals, notes of encouragement and resources from those who had walked this road before me.

As luck (or God) would have it, Laura lives in the Denver area. We became friends after Maisy's diagnosis and recovery and stayed in touch throughout the years. When Hope was born, I became a "repeat customer." Having support from Laura and String of Pearls was life-changing.

Regional Groups: I've appreciated getting involved in our local *Turner Syndrome* community, which provides opportunities to meet other families in the region who have this condition in common. I am grateful that Maisy can form relationships with her peers who will relate to her better than I can when it comes to certain shared experiences.

Resources and Connections I Found Less Helpful

"Something Similar": I was introduced to a number of friends of friends who had experienced "something similar," which often turned out to be a completely different diagnosis, outcome or situation. This might be comforting to some, but I didn't have the time or emotional energy to invest in learning about the whole spectrum of rare diseases.

Social Media Groups: I've found social media groups to be pretty unhelpful in general, especially if members are using the forum to ask other laypeople (myself included) for medical advice. That stresses me out—ask your doctor! I will occasionally consult a social media group to ask if something Maisy has experienced is known or common throughout the *Turner Syndrome* community, but I don't often engage in that forum. That said, some people love it (and not just for medical advice).

Events with a Broad "Target" Audience: Hope received hospice care through a phenomenal hospice organization, and we were invited to the organization's quarterly bereavement event. It was designed for all families who had lost a loved one and wanted to recognize them as part of this vigil.

Because this organization is not solely focused on pediatric hospice, I was concerned the majority of attendees would be remembering deceased elderly relatives. I politely declined because I thought this might become an isolating setting if we were the only ones grieving an infant. I could have been wrong about that, and I'm sure it was a lovely ceremony, but it didn't feel like a good fit or safe space for me at the time.

Setting boundaries (recall the diagram in Chapter Four) applies to your time and mental and emotional capacity for new information. Be judicious about how you want to focus your limited resources. And don't be afraid to politely decline a connection if it doesn't sound helpful. It might be helpful several months, years or decades from now, but it doesn't need to make your priority list today.

You've Met Grief, Too?

There was a common thread touching almost everyone who engaged with us most meaningfully during our season of utmost grief: They, too, had walked this lonely road of loss.

This reminds me of the thestrals in *Harry Potter*—the invisible horses that transport carriages from the train station to Hogwarts. Invisible, that is, until you've seen death. Once you've witnessed death, the horses—who you knew were real; they pulled your carriages and you heard their sounds—became visible to those in the "inner circle" of loss.

This is so true of my experience—those who knew loss were more primed to help. Was that because I was more likely to welcome them, knowing we shared a common burden? Or was that because they made fewer waves and more intuitively knew when to speak, when to stay silent and when I just needed a hug? It could have been both—who knows?

About two months after Hope passed, my friend Sarah brought a group of child loss club members together for a "grief lunch" where we could intentionally discuss topics that are generally taboo in the broader social context.

Some of my questions to this sacred circle:

- *What do you say when someone asks how many kids you have?*
- *Where is your child buried?*
- *How do you not just feel anxious all the time now?*
- *What is it like trying again to get pregnant after you've lost a child?*
- *Do you hang a stocking for your deceased child at Christmas?*
- *How has this loss impacted your other children and family members?*
- *What does it feel like when one, two, five years have passed?*

This grief lunch was actually much less depressing and much more cathartic than you might think.

It's refreshing to have a safe place to ask hard questions and to share deep hurts.

Does that mean intimate grief and loss circles have to be exclusive to the unfortunate card-carrying members? Absolutely not! Just because others haven't experienced the same losses doesn't mean they can't be a lifeline.

You Don't Have to be a Member to Shop Here

Here are two examples of how you might be an ally, even when the circumstance is completely foreign to you.

Example A

Several dear people in my life have gotten divorced in recent years. Because I've never personally experienced separation or divorce, I can empathize but not directly relate to the woes of infidelity, settlements, moving, lawyers-lawyers-lawyers, kid-swaps, job changes, financial shifts, "getting back out there" and all those things I can tell are zero percent fun.

No, I've never experienced this loss, but here's what I can apply from my own grief: "I'm so sorry. Would you like to go on a walk this weekend and chat more about it? I can't begin to imagine what you're going through, but I am familiar with the ache that comes when the dreams you had for your life start to crash to pieces, and it really sucks."

Example B

My brother Travis is dedicated to serving and praying for his teammates, neighbors, community and, really, anyone he meets. He engages regularly with a colleague whose adult son is battling cancer. It's been a year of weekly updates, highs, lows and unknowns.

He told me that engaging with this coworker each week has helped him care so much better for those experiencing cancer, even though he's never personally faced it. It's taught him to ask questions like: *Have you told your kids yet? What was that like for you—or what do you anticipate about that conversation?*

How insightful.

Let's try our best—holding empathy, respect and grace for one another. We might stub our toes along the way, but let's give it a whirl with great humility.

CHAPTER SEVEN

Speeds of Loss and Scales of Grief

In my experience, there are two relative speeds of loss and two relative scales of grief.

The Speeds of Loss

The first speed is fast—often too fast to digest. You feel it like a sucker punch or a blast of icy wind when it was supposed to be warm out today. That instant life-altering trauma that flashes before your eyes or burns itself into your memory when you get *the* phone call or *the* knock at the door.

The second speed is slow—sometimes excruciatingly slow. This comes in the form of watching your loved ones lose sanity to diseases like dementia, or diagnoses that take a while to unfold.

For us, Hope's life and death was slow burn grief.

I was nervous going to my 12-week ultrasound appointment for Hope given the news we received the last time we had an appointment like that. Even Kevin, Mr. Everything-Is-Okay-Always, was a bit nervous. But we thought, *We'll be fine. There's no way that will happen again.*

The ultrasound was going swimmingly—perfect heart tones, no fluid, typical size for gestational age. But our skilled sonographer couldn't get a great view of Hope's head and facial structure.

That day, we heard the word *holoprosencephaly* for the first time, but even still, I thought it was probably just a fluke and the next ultrasound would show no issues.

I left the OB's office and immediately called up my buddies at the children's hospital to see if I could get in that day for a follow-up ultrasound. The only perk to a second prenatal scare was that we were already VIPs at the hospital and knew who to see and what to expect, relatively speaking.

Less than three hours later, the results were confirmed. Hope's brain was malformed, and it was irreversible. There was nothing we did to cause it and nothing we could have done to prevent it. Just another unfortunate, random diagnosis. We'd either lose her soon or lose her…less soon.

That was April 24, 2023. I'll never forget the date because it was the day our sweet niece, Louisa, was born. She took her first breaths right as we received Hope's diagnosis. The circle of life and death always continues.

We followed the regular schedule of prenatal appointments. Every four to five weeks, we'd get an update on her growth, and we'd be able to see signs of her HPE a little more clearly: small (if any?) nose, bulbous eyes, cleft lip.

After about 20 weeks, doctors said that amazingly, my *womb of steel* (my words, not theirs) had done it again—created a happy home for a baby they thought would meet an early miscarriage. At that point, we shifted gears to start thinking about delivery.

My induction date was scheduled for October 31. Every day between July and October felt like I was holding my breath. I knew at some point in the next 12 or so weeks, a runaway train would come crashing through my house. I just didn't know what time, which direction it would come from, how fast it would move or how many casualties there would be. I was just alert—sometimes it felt like 24/7—waiting for the train to hit.

All the while, my precious baby grew inside me. And I loved her with all my heart. I knew these short days were the only ones I'd have with her.

On October 6, my water broke around 4:30 a.m., at 36 weeks gestation. I hadn't gone into labor naturally with Maisy, so I had no idea what to expect. It was nothing like you see in the movies—no two gallons of water rushing down my dress onto my Louboutins. But I knew enough to know this was it. The train, at long last (but also four weeks early!), was here.

Oddly, the delivery itself was much less stressful than Maisy's. There was a lot contributing to that: less ambiguity around Hope's condition, meaning that even though it was more severe, there were fewer unknowns; it was my second time going through this; it wasn't during COVID so I thankfully didn't have to wear a mask during labor this go-round; and the repeat hospital team fought so hard alongside me to help me achieve my delivery goals. After Hope arrived, her condition was stable enough to stay beside me in the hospital room without needing any treatment, even supplemental oxygen. By all accounts, miraculous.

Hope's two weeks were so short, yet so full. She spent practically every moment of her life in my arms or the arms of family members and friends and proud big sister, Maisy. Time stood still for all of us.

We brought her home on a Monday. On Wednesday, her skin sank to blue for the first time. We thought that was the end, but she made it ten more days. She was such a strong and beautiful girl. More on how we savored those two weeks later.

Hope passed peacefully on a Saturday, and we held her funeral a few days later. After her funeral, we invited close friends back to our home for queso and margaritas—the Havis way to mark any significant occasion.

It was oddly serene. Hope had lived a beautiful life full of love before passing peacefully. We had no regrets.

Finally that breath I'd been holding for months was released. I slept in anguish and sorrow but in peace. The train was gone, and we could start rebuilding, slowly but surely.

Talk about slow burn.

Two days after Hope's funeral, our generous neighbors invited us over for dinner to lighten our load. They cooked an amazing meal for us so we wouldn't have to worry about cooking or dishes.

After dinner, we were playing in their living room. Maisy was running back and forth across the room (as two-year-olds tend to do) when she bumped into our neighbor and knocked against the couch. In an instant, their dog, who had been lying docile on the couch, jumped up and bit Maisy on the face.

My gut twisted. I felt it in my whole self as it happened—the shock, fear, anger, dread. Kevin got to Maisy first, scooped her up and brought her to the sink. My first question: "Do I need to call 911?"

"Yes, immediately," Kevin said.

And call 911, I did. Between the blood and Kevin's reaction, I was afraid Maisy had lost an eye, finger or some other appendage. My heart still pumps fast as I think about it now. This is an example of the second speed of grief: that lightning fast give-anything-to-redo-that-moment speed.

In under five minutes, the ambulance had arrived, we'd collected our belongings and we were ready to hightail it to the hospital.

I'll spare you the gory details and other exasperating moments of that evening. Maisy was okay. All of her digits were intact and her eyeballs, too. The bite didn't puncture any nerves. It was *just* plastic surgery, a nasty scar, and some more trauma for my precious daughter to unravel in therapy for years to come.

A few snapshots I remember:

- ✦ Kevin telling the ER doc that if there was anything we could do to expedite, that would be appreciated…We just buried our other daughter two days ago. Yikes. She probably thought we were crazy.
- ✦ Looking at myself in the bathroom mirror at the ER. Stretchy postpartum pants. Blood splattered on my white puffer vest. Slow burn and speedy fast grief and trauma mingling into tears streaming down my face. Crying out to God, *What the ****? Now this? Why?*
- ✦ Thinking to myself, *Maisy's not going to die from this, so it's ultimately going to be okay.* Somehow, I was Captain Calm through this whole evening. Kevin almost passed out from the shock and

trauma to our innocent baby girl's precious skin that would never be undone. I was affected, too, but it turns out I'm becoming pretty good in a crisis. Thankfully, my mom was still in town after the funeral and sat with us and Maisy in the hospital all night long. I'm not sure how we would have made it through that night without her.

The breath I'd finally exhaled after Hope's funeral turned into hyperventilation less than 72 hours later.

I'd spent months preparing and processing and undergoing counseling to ready myself for Hope's arrival, which really did help cushion the blow. And then *boom*, my anxiety is at 11 (or maybe 50, on a scale of 1–10). And I'm looking around every corner wondering, *What's going to happen next?*

I write this story to illustrate the speeds of loss—fast and slow. Regardless of the speed, these losses tend to have a few commonalities:

Consumptive: Whether they become urgent priority #1 HOT NOW and ACT FAST or they require your steadfast love and caregiving for years to come, they become a big part of the story.

Expensive: Not only are they a big part of the story, but they also tend to claim a big part of the budget. Hospitals, surgeries, medical accessories, new dietary restrictions, nursing homes, medicines, new vehicles…these are costly.

Draining: Mentally, physically, emotionally, spiritually. There are new questions to wrestle with and new answers to find. There are likely 20 new Facebook groups waiting to greet you and engage with you on this topic…but will that even help? Or just add to your mental load, realizing you're new to this topic that others have been researching for years.

Demoralizing: A real hit to morale and hopefulness. What if we could rewind five little minutes to avoid this? Or skip out on that one-night camping trip that led to a lifelong battle with Lyme disease? Or take that extra vacation, not realizing it would be our last opportunity? Or just find a cure for cancer today, now, please?

The Scales of Grief

In addition to fast vs. slow loss, I've observed there are two primary types of grief: temporary setback vs. life-altering event.

I've talked enough about life-altering, devastating events: critical diagnoses, loss of a loved one, imprisonment, divorce, etc.

These are the ones that impact you to your core and fundamentally change your family—the ones you will remember for the rest of your life.

The "setback" category might include things like your newly finished basement flooding, hernia surgery, tedious car repairs, a mouthful of cavities that need to be filled—all of which I also experienced in the six months following Hope's death.

These things are also typically consumptive, expensive, draining and demoralizing bummers. But by the same time the next year, these setbacks will likely turn into distant memories and begrudging sighs, not life-altering moments.

That said, when these types of events occur, they are

annoying, painful and often costly. And it's okay to be upset about them.

This goes back to the idea of comparison. I often wonder if new moms are afraid to talk about "normal" baby problems around me because of my traumatic experiences with both of my pregnancies. I appreciate when they are cognizant that I would give anything to lose sleep to tend to Hope's newborn cries again…but at the same time, staying up all night with a newborn is exhausting and hard.

I remember being so overwhelmed when I was pregnant with Maisy, going through all the baby registry decisions for the first time. *Which stroller is best? What kind of bottle system do I need? What the heck is a breast pump, where do I get one and how do I learn how to use it?*

I found I was just as stressed out about choosing the "best" stroller brand as I was about selecting a heart surgeon. It's all relative! And it's okay to be stressed out about a stroller brand even if you're not worrying about an open-heart surgery. By the way, I made great selections for the surgeon and the stroller brand (not trying to start a stroller war here).

Zoom out even further and these are all problems of privilege. I've had an ultrasound. I can afford a stroller.

The hospital where I delivered was not in a war zone.

You see what I mean? We can always make the scale of issues bigger or smaller. I do think it's important to keep a healthy perspective of our relative scale of grief and pain, but all we can do is embrace the challenges in front of us, not focus on everyone else's challenges, other than to offer help when we can. And perspective goes hand-in-hand with gratitude.

CHAPTER EIGHT

Practice Gratitude

There's always something to be grateful for, even in the midst of really hard days. I encourage you to find something to be grateful for each day. Not in a way that dismisses your grief, but in a way that gives you perspective and a shred of light in the dark valley.

Practicing gratitude works best when it comes from within you.

As I've already discussed ad nauseam, someone else saying "at least X, Y, Z" typically sparks annoyance rather than gratitude. This also applies when it truly feels warranted...like the mom complaining about breastfeeding when all you're trying to do is keep your baby alive. But even then, the "at least" comments are typically not helpful, for me or that mom.

It works best when you look in the mirror and feed yourself a healthy dose of perspective.

Can you relate to any of these?

- *I'm thankful I have a loving family.*
- *I'm thankful there's a roof over my head.*
- *I'm thankful I'm not trapped in a burning building.*
- *I'm thankful I have a job even though it feels super stressful.*
- *I'm thankful for doctors who know what they're doing.*
- *I'm thankful my neighbors brought banana bread.*
- *I'm thankful my kids are safe.*
- *I'm thankful I can watch my favorite movie tonight, just because.*
- *I'm thankful the dog didn't eat too much and throw up today.*

- *I'm thankful my computer turned on today.*
- *I'm thankful for time to listen to that podcast.*
- *I'm thankful that even though pretty much everything else hurts, my elbows are feeling pretty good today. Let's go, elbows!*

Have you ever met someone who gives off "Eeyore" vibes? No matter what happens, there's always something to complain about? I used to think Eeyore people were just destined to be that way, or that they really did have it tougher than everyone else.

Meanwhile, I attributed my general positivity to my natural disposition and pervasively positive experiences and privileges. But I've also been through some hard stuff. And it's shown me that gratitude is most certainly a choice. And it's a delight to be around people who choose to be thankful, regardless of their circumstances, rather than people who can't—or won't—let go of disappointment and bitterness.

It takes practice. I am not an expert, but I am learning. If you're feeling brave, find someone to hold you accountable to gratitude—even on your darkest days. This person might drive you crazy sometimes, but they will also drive you to be a better person.

Post-Traumatic Growth

You've likely heard of Post-Traumatic Stress Disorder (PTSD), which is an all too common disorder caused by exposure to traumatic events. When triggered, those suffering from PTSD will face immense physical or emotional distress, hearkening back to the initial traumatic event.

As I was preparing for Hope's birth, I met with a psychiatrist, Dr. Buxton (Dr. B for short). After listening to the story of Maisy's birth and her first tumultuous and amazing two years of life, Dr. B introduced me to the concept of *Post-Traumatic Growth.*

Similar to PTSD, Post-Traumatic Growth starts with a jarring event. However, instead of experiencing continued distress, new, healthy roots begin to form. And if you bring gratitude and community into your life, this trauma can eventually make you a more grounded and resilient individual. This is by no means a call for faking positivity or minimizing traumatic events. It's not a fix-all or even a great consolation prize, but it does resonate with my experience: A good salve for trauma is gratitude plus human connection. And with the right nutrients, your life can become a place where blooms begin to flourish anew.

A Note on Levity and Time Well Spent

When Hope was at home with us, I spent hours every morning staring at her, trying to latch on to every single detail of her person: from her delicate dimples, to her soft skin, to her gentle stretches. I spent time praying with her and singing to her. And of course, I spent time crying, telling her how much I would miss her.

And then the clock would hit nine a.m.

I was so intentional about making the most of our time together. I didn't want to miss a single moment of meaning in her short life. And what a gift it was to watch and savor every breath.

But, it turns out, you—or at least, I—can only be so reflective and grievous and solemn for so many hours of the day. There is a physical limit to somberness, and I maxed out around six hours per day.

The other hours of the day? I went about my daily life—with Hope, of course. We watched cheesy rom-coms together. We read books together. We went on walks together. We enjoyed meals together. We played with Maisy together. We danced together. We spent time with family together. We invited friends into our home together. We laughed and cried together.

Virtually nothing felt like a waste! We were together, doing everyday life.

Important side note: The only thing that did feel like a waste was social media. I thought to myself, *If I look down from my doomscroll to see she has died in my arms at this moment, I would regret it.* Thankfully, that did not happen. For you, the answer to "what would feel like a waste" might be different, so it's a good thing to consider.

All the moments we spent together doing normal things, not hyper-sacred or somber things, felt like a perfect use of time and has given me great confidence in how I spend my days. I don't have to wonder how I would spend time if I knew my life was nearing its end. I've had a glimpse of that, and nothing significant changed. What a gift of perspective I have received because of Hope.

CHAPTER NINE

So, What Am I Not Supposed To Say at a Funeral?

Supporting those who grieve takes practice. It's a sport no one wants to be good at, but those who have mastered it are sacred refuges.

I'm certainly not claiming to be a professional. I've made my fair share of blunders.

I recently attended the first funeral I'd been to since Hope's. My friend's grandmother passed away, and I attended to show support. At the funeral, I ran into her sister who greeted me and said, "Hi, how are you?"

To my horror, I responded, "Doing well, thanks! How are you?"

I immediately clapped my hand to my mouth. "Wow, that was a dumb thing to say. Of course you're not doing well," was my next *inspired* sentiment. "I'm so sorry for your loss..."

And that's coming from me, a person authoring a book about what not to say at a funeral. It's not easy out here, folks. And like I said, it takes practice. And grace.

What To Say at a Funeral

So, what *do* you say at a funeral?

First of all, start by showing up. If you are invited to a funeral and can arrange your schedule to attend, I encourage you to do so. I can tell you it means the world.

The fact that people chose to attend Hope's funeral said more to me than words ever could. I can still tell you, by name, all the neighbors and coworkers who attended the services. I didn't keep track so I could look down on those who didn't attend—it just meant so much to me that those people, some merely acquaintances, chose to spend an hour of their day honoring Hope's life with us.

When I returned to work and thanked these

coworkers again for coming to Hope's funeral, I quickly observed a pattern. The colleagues who weren't close personal friends all had something in common: They, too, had lost someone they loved, and they remembered what it meant when people showed up at the funeral.

In the post-funeral receiving line, those who had walked with me through the journey didn't even need to say anything; their hugs were all I needed. A lot of people said, "I'm sorry for your loss," which I think is absolutely acceptable and appropriate.

The comment that meant most to me was simple: "You were a great mom." I still get chills and tears thinking of those words from a lifelong family friend, Brian. How did he know that was my greatest desire—to be a great mom to Hope for her short life?

Five words. One syllable fewer than "I'm sorry for your loss," and yet those words resonated deep into my core. You. Were. A. Great. Mom.

I was sharing this with my friend Adam, who was relatively young when he lost his father. Adam told me that even ten years later, the comment that sticks with him the most from his dad's funeral was, "Twenty-nine is too young to lose a parent."

These statements are simple and true. They are heartfelt and genuine. They are personal and reverberant.

What <u>To</u> Say and Do at a Funeral

Hopefully, you've picked up tips throughout this book about truly supportive ways to approach those experiencing grief and loss.

For those scanning to the end of the book before tomorrow's funeral, here's a cheat sheet:

- *Do go to the funeral! Show up and sign the guest book.*
- *Do say something.*
- *Do keep it short and sweet.*
- *Do offer a hug.*
- *Do make whatever you say personal and true.*
- *It's okay to make someone laugh by sharing a happy memory (at least if that someone is like me).*

What <u>Not</u> To Say and Do at a Funeral

- ⊗ *Don't make it about you or your experiences.*
- ⊗ *Don't say "Everything happens for a reason."*
- ⊗ *Don't say "at least…"*
- ⊗ *Don't minimize the loss or grief.*
- ⊗ *Don't overthink it.*

If you are stumped, here are a few generally safe things to say:

- *I'm so sorry.*
- *I'm here for you always.*
- *You look so beautiful, and I'm just so sorry for your loss.*
- *It's an honor to grieve with you. Your loved one will be greatly missed.*
- *I'm so glad I can be here with your family today as we remember your loved one.*

Obviously, everyone's situation is different. Maybe the griever was estranged from the deceased. Maybe the loss came in the form of a tragic accident, a swirl of unknown or the despair of suicide or violence.

There's never an easy funeral. And there's no way to write a textbook that can capture what to say in each particular situation. But starting with genuine care and simple observations of truth will steer you in the right direction.

And if you don't have something nice to say, just stick with, "I'm sorry for your loss."

CHAPTER TEN

Gifts, Memories and Other Ideas

I look back with gratitude at the many family members, friends, caregivers, neighbors and coworkers who stood by us during Hope's diagnosis, brief life and death. Below are some tangible examples of how people showed up for us—and how you might consider showing up for others.

Memories I Treasure

- Hours after receiving Hope's diagnosis, our dear friends and leaders in our church, James and Sarah, dropped everything and came to our house to pray with us and bring us dinner. They came to listen and cry with us and did not offer any grand platitudes to "ease" our pain.

- Instead of a baby shower, my friend Lillie and a few other close friends organized a special evening where they showered me with love. They made my favorite dinner, gave me meaningful gifts, wrote words of encouragement and listened and prayed as I shared my hopes and fears.

- When Hope made her midnight debut, I sent up a flare and our crew came running. None of us knew at the time that Hope would be well enough to leave the hospital, so we brought the welcome party to her. My parents and Kevin's parents arrived with a bleary-eyed Maisy. James led a bedside baptism. Sarah delivered a blanket, knitted by a circle of ladies from church. Lillie captured all these moments in beautiful photos.

- While Hope was with us, my friend Meghan drove by just about every other day to drop off food and gifts (including treats for our dog, who was definitely neglected during that time). She would text me and say, "I left some food on your porch! I'm nearby if you need a hug!" Her five-minute visits were so special. And it means so much to me that she got to hold Hope during those drop-by visits.

Memorabilia I Treasure

- Photos from our newborn shoot and at-home photo shoot—some of the only photos I will ever have of Hope.
- A shadow box I created with the hat Hope wore, cards stamped with her handprints and footprints, and other treasured items that remind me of her.
- Gifts from the hospital, including a wooden frame with Hope's footprints engraved and a necklace charm with Hope's fingerprint stamped on it.
- A canvas with all four of our handprints on it, prominently displayed next to canvas prints of our family photos.
- Custom jewelry with Hope's name engraved or birthstone represented.

- ✦ Personalized holiday ornaments.
- ✦ A song written by our friend Ian titled, "Dear Hope" that he and Kevin played during Hope's memorial service. It's such a beautiful tribute I love to revisit.
- ✦ A candle Kevin's friends made with pictures of Hope printed on its glass holder. We light it on special occasions as we remember her.

So many people reached out with kind words, brought us meals and sent us flowers and other gifts.

Beyond the initial loss, one way you can continue to engage with people you care about is to remember anniversaries of tough days—birthdays, death days, divorce days, particularly lonesome holidays and others. It means a lot when others remember you and your lost loved ones.

Final Thoughts

If I could sum up all my advice into a single (if rather long and clunky) sentence, it would go something like this:

Find real community; go to the funeral; show up and listen; say something genuine (without the words "at least"); don't make it about you; offer a hug.

But I think the Golden Rule says it even better:

Do for others what you would want to be done for you.

SPECIAL ACKNOWLEDGMENT

Of all the incredible people who have come alongside us, one stands out as an exemplar of grief guidance (what a title!): our dear friend, Laura, who founded the perinatal hospice organization String of Pearls I mentioned earlier.

Laura retired in 2023, and we were one of her final families. It turns out Hope's diagnosis of *alobar holoprosencephaly* was the exact same as Pearl's (Laura's deceased daughter).

Laura spent 16 years serving thousands of families through some of their hardest moments. Since Laura and I had the luxury of living in the same metro area, I got to meet with her regularly throughout my journey with Hope.

She is a person shaped by grief and carrying the griefs of others—and she's a pro. She knows exactly when to show up, when to give space, when to bring dinner (and always breakfast for the next morning!) and when to provide resources like birth plans, baby burial shopping lists and keepsakes for when the baby is born. Her care was truly a godsend and her presence was always welcomed.

When I went to visit and hold Hope's body for the last time before her burial, Laura told me she'd meet me at the funeral home. I told her that wasn't necessary—Kevin and I just wanted some time alone with Hope. She didn't come in with us. She just sat in her car. For an hour. But as I said an impossible goodbye to Hope, I felt so much relief knowing I would walk out the doors of the funeral home and get a much-needed hug from a trusted friend.

She sat. And she waited.

That's it! How can it be so simple? And yet…who would think of that? Certainly not I, before that day. But now, I know how much it means.

I don't know many people who can spend their days in the sacred space between death and life, life and death. The precious few, like Laura and our hospice team, sit in the in-between and have practiced these moments. We would do well to learn much from them.

ENDNOTES

1. Page 4: “What is Holoprosencephaly (HPE)?,” (Birth Defect Research for Children website), https://birthdefects.org/holoprosencephaly/.

2. Page 15: Mattie Aguero, “Evolution of American Funerary Customs and Laws," (Library of Congress, September 28, 2022), https://blogs.loc.gov/law/2022/09/evolution-of-american-funerary-customs-and-laws/.

3. Page 15: “With Malice Towards None: The Abraham Lincoln Bicentennial Exhibition, Lincoln's Long Journey Home,” (Library of Congress Exhibits), https://www.loc.gov/exhibits/lincoln/interactives/long-journey-home/apr_24/index.html.

4. Page 15: “How the Funeral Industry has Evolved,” (FuneralWise.com), https://www.funeralwise.com/resources/funeral-industry/.

5. Page 15: Mattie Aguero, “Evolution of American Funerary Customs and Laws," (Library of Congress, September 28, 2022), https://blogs.loc.gov/law/2022/09/evolution-of-american-funerary-customs-and-laws/.

6. Page 16: Jeff Burtka, “Burial and Cremation Laws in Colorado,” (Nolo.com, September 10, 2024), https://www.nolo.com/legal-encyclopedia/burial-cremation-laws-colorado.html.

7. Page 17: Rabbi Malka Michel, “What to Do and What to Expect at a Shiva,” (ExploringJudaism.org), https://exploringjudaism.org/living/what-to-do-and-what-to-expect-at-a-shiva/. Page 17: Zalman Goldstein, “Shloshim - The 30-day Mourning Period,” (Chabad.org), https://www.chabad.org/library/article_cdo/aid/371240/jewish/The-Shloshim.htm.

8. Page 17: Zalman Goldstein, “Kaddish in Hebrew & English: Mourner's Kaddish & Kaddish D'Rabanan,” (Chabad.org), https://www.chabad.org/library/article_cdo/aid/371110/jewish/Kaddish-in-Hebrew-English.htm.

9. Page 17: “Food & Condolence Baskets, Shiva Gifts,” (shiva.com), https://www.shiva.com/learning-center/what-to-bring-or-send/food-condolence-baskets. “Sitting Shiva,” (shiva.com), https://www.shiva.com/learning-center/sitting-shiva.

10. Page 17: “Did You Know? Trisagion Service,” (Greek Orthodox Archdiocese of America website, July 16, 2024), https://www.goarch.org/-/dyk-trisagion.

11. Page 17: “A Complete Guide to Traditional Chinese Funeral Customs,” (DiginityMemorial.com), hhttps://www.dignitymemorial.com/memorial-services/funeral-traditions/chinese-funeral-traditions. Liu Jue, “How Did Ancient Chinese Mourn the Deceased?” (TheWorldOfChinese.com, April 5, 2022), https://www.theworldofchinese.com/2022/04/how-did-ancient-chinese-mourn-the-deceased/.

ACKNOWLEDGMENTS

What Not To Say at a Funeral is one big thank you note to the people in my life who continually show up when it matters most.

To the Left Field Publishing team: Kristen, thank you for believing in me from day one. I owe so much of this to you and Len. Thank you also to Cameron and Grace for the incisive edits.

To our healthcare providers: Thank you for everything. Maisy is alive because of you. Hope had a beautiful entry into the world because of you.

To first readers and early champions: Thank you for every edit, question and word of encouragement. To Courtney: Thank you for making this real!

To our community of family, friends, neighbors and coworkers: Thank you for the meals and tea parties and honest questions and open arms. Life is better because of you.

To Mom, Dad, Enid and Charlie: Thank you for being present. What a bond we forged because of Hope.

To Kevin: Thank you for your constant encouragement and partnership. You are the best hubby to me and dad to our girlies. I love you!

To Maisy, Hope, and now Annie: I'm so very blessed and thankful to be your mom. You are my heart.

ABOUT THE AUTHOR

Amy Havis leverages her background as a communications strategist to share a practical perspective about how people navigate difficult conversations and life's hardest moments. After experiencing profound personal loss, Amy became a passionate advocate for replacing silence with presence and connection. Her writing invites us to show up—at home, at work and in grief—with honesty, empathy and heart. She lives in Colorado with her family. *What Not To Say at a Funeral* is her first book. Visit her at www.AmyHavisAuthor.com

DISCUSSION QUESTIONS

1. *Was there a moment in this book where you felt particularly seen or understood? What was happening for you as you read it?*

2. *What do you notice about yourself right now, having reached the end of this book?*

3. *Have you ever been unsure what to say—or whether to say anything at all—when someone was grieving? How did this book challenge or affirm that instinct?*

4. *What phrases or responses have you heard in times of loss that felt unhelpful or painful? What might you say—or not say—differently now?*

5. *Where do you see yourself in this book: more often as the person grieving, or the person trying to support? How does that shape the way you read it?*

6. *What does showing up well look like to you after reading this book?*

7. *What do you feel less pressure to get "right" than you did before?*

8. *How do you tend to respond to grief—your own or others'? Through action, silence, humor, avoidance, fixing or something else?*

9. *Is there someone in your life right now who might need gentler presence rather than better words? What could that look like in practice now that you've read the book?*

10. *If you could offer one sentence of compassion—to yourself or someone else—what would you say today?*

WHAT *NOT* TO SAY AT A FUNERAL

- ⊗ *Don't say, "Everything happens for a reason."*
- ⊗ *Don't say, "At least…"*
- ⊗ *Don't say, "When I was in your shoes..."*
- ⊗ *Don't say, "It could have been worse..."*
- ⊗ *Don't say, "It's okay. God's got a plan."*
- ⊗ *Don't say, "This will make you stronger."*
- ⊗ *Don't say, "God doesn't give things we can't handle, so you must be able to handle it."*
- ⊗ *Don't say, "I know exactly how you feel.."*
- ⊗ *Don't minimize the loss or grief.*
- ⊗ *Don't overthink it.*
- ⊗ *Don't make it about you or your experiences.*

WHAT *TO* SAY AT A FUNERAL

- *Do say, "I'm so sorry you're going through this. Is it okay if I give you a hug?"*
- *Do say, "I'm here for you always."*
- *Do say, "It's an honor to grieve with you. Your loved one will be greatly missed."*
- *Do say, "I'm so glad I can be here with today as we remember your loved one."*
- *Do say something.*
- *Do go to the funeral! Show up and sign the guest book.*
- *Do keep it short and sweet.*
- *Do make whatever you say personal and true.*
- *It's okay to make someone laugh by sharing a happy memory (at least if that someone is like me).*

ABOUT THE PUBLISHER

LEFT FIELD PUBLISHING–where creativity meets collaboration. We're a forward-thinking publishing company created to combine the best attributes of traditional publishing with the best attributes of independent publishing. We exist to help authors bring their work to market in a cost-effective way while allowing them to retain control over their writing projects.

Our vision is to reimagine what publishing can be—bold, collaborative, and purpose-driven—by amplifying genre-defying voices across fiction, non-fiction, YA and kids books. Because great books aren't defined by a category.

Visit us at www.Left-Field-Publishing.com.

Connect with us!

Facebook: /leftfieldpublishing
Instagram: @leftfieldpublishing
TikTok: leftfieldpublishing
YouTube: @LeftFieldPublishing-m4g
LinkedIn: Left Field Publishing

READERS COLLECTIVE

Join the Left Field Publishing Readers Collective!

Where passionate readers become part of the publishing revolution

- Adopt an Author
- Participate in Left Field Book Clubs
- Join a Street Team
- Influence What We Publish
- Read & Review
- & More!

JOIN NOW @ www.Left-Field-Publishing.com

READERS COLLECT